# MARTY'S ROADTRIP

### Patricia D. Ensing
### Illustrations by Blueberry Illustrations

Copyright © 2020 by Patricia D. Ensing

All rights reserved.
No part of this book may be reproduced
or transmitted in any form or by any means
without written permission from the author.

Library of Congress Control Number: 2020903196

ISBN: 978-1-7361707-0-0

**This book is dedicated to** my adventurous, loving, and supportive husband, Bill, our daughters Buffy and Heather, our son-in-law Joey, and our grandsons Joseph, Justin, Jeremiah, and Jared. This book could not have been written without the love, support, and editing from my dear friend Jill, the encouragement from my friends Marcia and Janet, and the lovely garden belonging to our neighbors and friends Cynthia and Peter.

Also, a huge thank you to Marty for taking this adventure with us and making this book possible. Every time we see a monarch butterfly, we all say, "Hi, Marty!"

My name is Marty. I am a beautiful monarch butterfly.
I have not always been a butterfly though.
You just have to hear what happened
to me while on a car road trip.

First, I was a small egg on a leaf of a milkweed plant in a field of flowers in Door County, Wisconsin. Then in a short time I became a caterpillar.

One day, while I was sitting on a milkweed leaf munching away, a farmer who grew the flowers hand-picked the flower of the milkweed plant with me still on it. I ended up in a vase with other flowers to be sold at his flower stand.

The very next day a man and woman (who became my friends) bought the vase of flowers I was in and put it in their car. This was when my adventure began.

I had seen cars drive past the farm, but I had never been in a car before. I sat on the leaf very still and

saw fields with cows, sheep, and horses as we drove down the highway. It was a bright, sunny day with a beautiful blue sky.

After a very long car ride,
we came to their home in Illinois.

They put the vase of flowers on a table inside their home.

They did not know I was on a leaf inside the vase, so when I peeked out they were delighted to see a cute, furry caterpillar. Me! I had new friends!

After a few days, I became familiar with my new "inside" home, and I decided to go for a walk. I crawled off the milkweed leaf onto a very slippery wooden table and slid across it. Wheeeeee! That was fun! Then I crawled up on a soft sofa. It was so comfortable that I soon fell asleep.

I'm not sure how long I napped but all of a sudden, I woke up in my friend's hand. I was so thankful she found me, because there was no milkweed on that comfy sofa and that's all I eat. Phew!

She gently placed me back on the milkweed leaf but I was in a different vase with a soft airy cover. My new vase was placed near the window and I could look out to see flowers, trees, squirrels, birds, and butterflies.

One day I felt my body beginning to change. I was hanging on the milkweed branch by a thin silk string. My shape started to look like the letter J, and I was no longer hungry.

But I was not in this J-shape very long! My body changed again into a beautiful light green cocoon with pretty gold dots at the top and at the bottom.

My friends decided to go on another long car ride to visit their daughter in Pennsylvania. I was happy they took me along with them so I would not be alone. Getting around in a car was beginning to be fun. The road was bumpy but I was fine in my safe cocoon in the vase.

This road trip seemed longer than the last one, but I enjoyed it very much. Along the way I saw trees, ponds, birds, bridges, and buildings,

But this is when my story becomes a little unusual. You see, all monarch butterflies go through these changes, but I don't think they go on vacation. Here's what happened to me next.

I was a little startled when I realized that their daughter had two furry animals that ran all around the house. There was a dog named Jennie, who barked a lot, and a big fat cat named Gables. They ignored

me and I ignored them. I was glad that my friends' home in Illinois did not have these animals. I am not sure what would have happened if they had found me sleeping on the sofa. Yikes!

One night, while my friends and pets were all asleep,

my cocoon suddenly opened and I wiggled out. I saw that I had amazing black and gold wings just like other monarch butterflies I had seen through the big windows. It was so exciting!

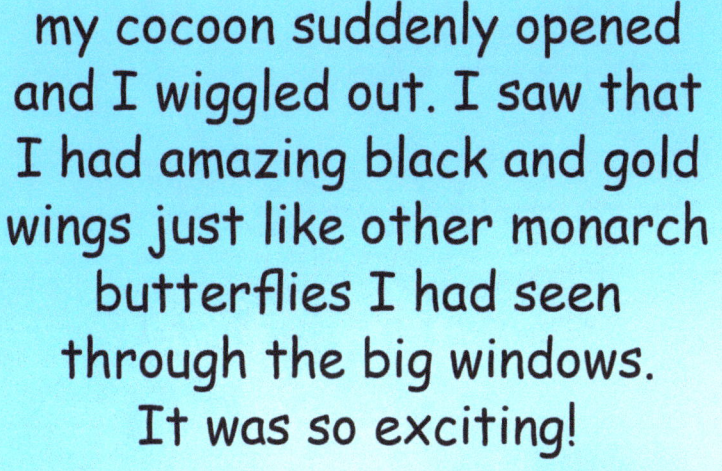

I was so surprised to learn that when I moved my wings faster, I would lift off the branch even though I was still in the vase. It was so thrilling!

The next day, my friends put my vase and me back into their car to go on another long car ride back to their home in Illinois. Even though I was ready to fly on my own, they wanted me to go home with them. I was happy to stay with them to enjoy another car ride.

When we arrived in Illinois, they took me to visit their neighbor's home who had an amazing garden full of beautiful trees and flowers.

After they gently placed my vase on the ground, they lifted the cover and I flew high up into the air. Wow!

Whoa! I could really fly with these beautiful black and gold wings!

I landed on a branch near the top of a tall tree and looked down at my friends and their neighbors. Flying is amazing! Now I know why people use cars to get around. They don't have wings!

I realized that it was time to say goodbye to my friends. I said thank you in my own way by dipping and waving my wings. They did not see me because I was so high up in the tree.

After they all went into their neighbor's home, I flew back down to enjoy the beautiful garden.

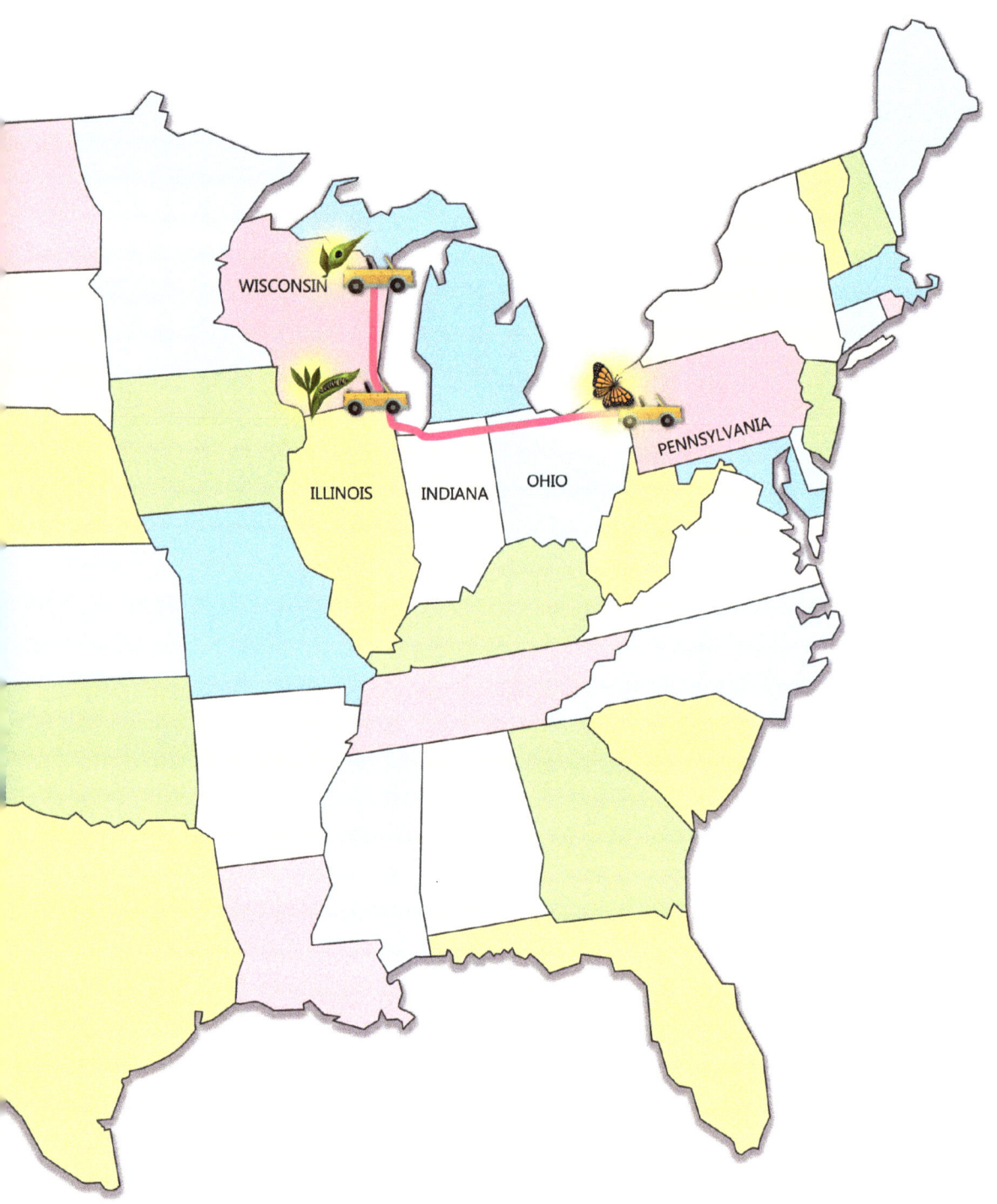

I'm very grateful they took me along on their road trips. I would have become a monarch butterfly on the farm in Wisconsin but wouldn't have had the exciting road trips with them in their car.

I may fly into your garden one day.
Look for me. I will definitely look for you.

**Patricia D. Ensing is** a wife, a mother of two daughters, a mother-in law, grandmother to four grandsons, a sister, and an aunt. She lives in a northern suburb of Chicago, Illinois. She enjoys her church and being with family and friends. She likes to read, take road trips, cook, and she loves nature. This is her first children's book, with more books to follow.